MIX
Papier aus verantwortungsvollen Quellen
Paper from responsible sources
FSC® C105338

Anna Laeser

Managing Culture Clashes in M&A's

Anchor Academic
Publishing

Laeser, Anna: Managing Culture Clashes in M&A's. Hamburg, Anchor Academic Publishing 2013

Buch-ISBN: 978-3-95489-152-8
PDF-eBook-ISBN: 978-3-95489-652-3
Druck/Herstellung: Anchor Academic Publishing, Hamburg, 2013

Bibliografische Information der Deutschen Nationalbibliothek:
Die Deutsche Nationalbibliothek verzeichnet diese Publikation in der Deutschen Nationalbibliografie; detaillierte bibliografische Daten sind im Internet über http://dnb.d-nb.de abrufbar.

All rights reserved. This publication may not be reproduced, stored in a retrieval system or transmitted, in any form or by any means, electronic, mechanical, photocopying, recording or otherwise, without the prior permission of the publishers.

Das Werk einschließlich aller seiner Teile ist urheberrechtlich geschützt. Jede Verwertung außerhalb der Grenzen des Urheberrechtsgesetzes ist ohne Zustimmung des Verlages unzulässig und strafbar. Dies gilt insbesondere für Vervielfältigungen, Übersetzungen, Mikroverfilmungen und die Einspeicherung und Bearbeitung in elektronischen Systemen.

Die Wiedergabe von Gebrauchsnamen, Handelsnamen, Warenbezeichnungen usw. in diesem Werk berechtigt auch ohne besondere Kennzeichnung nicht zu der Annahme, dass solche Namen im Sinne der Warenzeichen- und Markenschutz-Gesetzgebung als frei zu betrachten wären und daher von jedermann benutzt werden dürften.

Die Informationen in diesem Werk wurden mit Sorgfalt erarbeitet. Dennoch können Fehler nicht vollständig ausgeschlossen werden und der Diplomica Verlag, die Autoren oder Übersetzer übernehmen keine juristische Verantwortung oder irgendeine Haftung für evtl. verbliebene fehlerhafte Angaben und deren Folgen.

Alle Rechte vorbehalten

© Anchor Academic Publishing, Imprint der Diplomica Verlag GmbH
Hermannstal 119k, 22119 Hamburg
http://www.diplomica-verlag.de, Hamburg 2013
Printed in Germany

Table of Contents

List of Abbreviations I
List of Figures II
Management Summary III

1 **Introduction** 1
    1.1 Overview of the M&A Market and Activity 1
    1.2 Problem Statement 2
    1.3 Research Method 3
    1.4 Structure 3

2 **Definitions** 4
    2.1 Transactions and Due Diligence 4
    2.2 Culture and Culture Clashes 5
    2.3 Trust and Language 8

3 **Impact of M&A's** 9
    3.1 In General 9
    3.2 During the M&A Stages 9
    3.3 Cultural Problems and Key Drivers in M&A Stages 11

4 **Integration Models as Solution Alternatives** 12
    4.1 Analysis Approach 12
    4.2 Selection of Existing Integration Models 12
        4.2.1 The Delta Model by Faber 12
        4.2.2 The Three Phase Model by Wollersheim 14
        4.2.3 The Three Phase Model by Schneck 14
        4.2.4 The Three Phase Model by Schuler 15
        4.2.5 The Organizational Fit by Cartwright 15
        4.2.6 The Customized CDD Model by Carleton 16
        4.2.7 The Three Phase Framework by Trompenaars 18
        4.2.8 Various Supplemental Models and Studies 18
    4.3 Evaluation of the Models 20

| 5 | A Set of Cultural Integration Tools | 23 |

6	Conclusion	26
	6.1 Summary and Conclusion	26
	6.2 Outlook and Recommendations	27

Appendices IV
References XIV
Other Bibliography XVIII

List of Abbreviations

Bn	Billion
CDD	Cultural Due Diligence
CL	Checklist
e.g.	exempli gratia (for example)
DD	Due Diligence
HR	Human Resources
IDV	Individualism versus Collectivism
IT	Information Technology
KPI	Key Performance Indicator
LTO	Long-Term versus Short-Term Orientation
MAS	Masculinity versus Femininity
M&A's	Mergers and Acquisitions
OVP	Organizational Value Profiler
PD	Power Distance
PVP	Personal Value Profiler
R&D	Research and Development
UA	Uncertainty Avoidance
US$	US Dollar

List of Figures

Figure 1. Key drivers for M&As 1

Figure 2. Due Diligence Types 5

Figure 3. Key Differences by Basic Culture Problem 6

Figure 4. Culture Problem Indices by Country 7

Figure 5. Human Due Diligence Delta Model 13

Figure 6. Cultural Due Diligence Assessment 17

Figure 7. Process for Capturing Value 20

Figure 8. Comparison of Existing Integration Models 21

Figure 9. The Cultural Integration Toolkit 24

Management Summary

Merger and acquisition activities have become an integral part of today's businesses world. They are considered as strategic component to gain market share and extend product portfolios. Still, these transactions have a huge impact on an organization. This paper looks specifically at the M&A impact on company culture. Based on an analysis of identified key elements, which drive an M&A process, a cultural integration toolkit will be developed to solve identified cultural problems. Secondary data serves as source data for an inductive approach. Cultural problems and key drivers will be identified based on systematic research. The implantation of these key drivers in existing integration models will be further studied. Findings prove that not all of the identified key drivers are implemented in the models. Therefore, existing models solve the identified cultural problems semi-efficient. This leaves the need for a basic integration tool, which implements all key drivers, serves as guideline through an M&A process and provides specific instruments for realization of single steps. This paper develops such a basic integration toolkit in chapter 5. The toolkit meets all these requirements and proves that "managing culture clashes in M&A's" is possible.

1 Introduction

1.1 Overview of the M&A Market and Activity

The focus of this paper is on merger and acquisition (M&A) activity. It starts with an overview of global M&A deal volumes. Mergermarket shows in their "Round-up for Year End 2011" an increase of global M&A deal values from 1,600 US$ bn in 2004 to 3,600 US$ bn in 2007. In the period from 2007 to 2009 the global deal value dropped to 1,600 US$ bn and leveled out since 2010 at around 2,000 US$ bn (mergermarket, 2012, p. 3). This deal activity leads to the question for key drivers which are discussed in several KPMG studies and other publications (KPMG, 1999, p. 8; KPMG, 2008, p. 8; KPMG, 2011, p. 8; Schuler, 2001; p. 240; Harding, 2004, p. 123; Bower, 2001, p. 94; Bech, 2007, pp. 18-28).

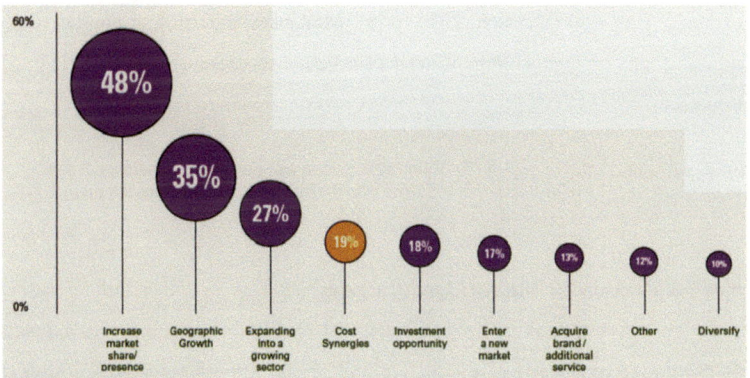

Figure 1.Key drivers for M&As
(Source: KPMG, 2011, p. 8)

The above shown extract of a KPMG study names as acquisition strategies: increase of market share, geographical growth, expanding into growing sectors, cost synergies, investment opportunities, entering new markets, acquiring brand (KPMG, 2011, p. 8). Schuler adds further strategies such as

> "acquisition of cash, [...] bigger asset base to leverage borrowing, [...] gaining core competence [...], talent / knowledge and technology [...]" (Schuler, 2001, p. 240).

There are many rationales behind M&A's creating different challenges. M&A transactions cause a *"fight for control"* (Bower, 2001, p. 94) between the executive groups and manager groups of both companies, especially when equal companies merge. This leads to slowing down the decision making process and interrupting the due diligence and integration process. Cross border M&A's face *"cultural and governmental differences"* (Bower, 2001, p. 94) slowing down specific legal due diligence steps. CEO's pointed out in a roundtable meeting, that they tried to lay out the management structure, others started with their integration work by the time the acquisition was planned, and a few stated that communication is the key (Carey, 2001, p. 15). A wide variety of challenges comes along when M&A's are planned and executed. They have a huge impact on the new organization, its strategies, structures, cultures and many other components. That requires a solid planning of M&A activities expressed in success measures. These are typically share price, market share, customer service levels and satisfaction, profitability, productivity, staff motivation and morale (Carleton, 2004, pp. 9-12). Deloitte has used some of these success measures to create risk areas to further examine failure rates of M&A transactions by four risk areas. The study evaluated data from Europe, America and Asia over six years and resulted in an average failure rate of 72.5% of all investigated M&A's (Gerds, 2010, pp. 72-76). A McKinsey study from 2010 stated M&A failure rates of 66-75% as well (Deutsch, 2010, p. 5). McKinsey indicated in another study that many acquirers focus on cost savings instead of revenue increase. (Bekier, 2001, p. 3). The Vector Group sees

> "(1) failure to assess the potential impact of attempting to merge and integrate the cultures of the companies involved and (2) failure to plan for systemic and systematic and efficient integration [...]"

as the two major basic reason for M&A failure (Carleton, 2004, p. 1). Other failure reasons are named, but not exclusively, as draining financials, underestimating transition costs, power and politics as driving force instead of productive and organizational objectives, losing or mismanaging talent and totally different management styles (Schuler, 2001, p. 241; Carey, 2001, p. 12). Communicaid showed that 45% of M&A failures result from "unexpected post deal people problems" (Communicaid, 2011, p. 2). Increased internal focus leads to lack of focus on customers, low motivation and the loss of key staff and executives create enormous inefficiencies through loss of time – and *"just have to be lived through"* (Carleton, 2004, p. 15).

1.2 Problem Statement

The high failure rates signal a need for more awareness for and guidance through the integration process. While some M&A research areas study hard facts others scan soft issues and their impact on the organizational structure which affects long-term performance. This paper concentrates on culture clash specifically.

The purpose of this paper is to examine the correlation between cultural issues and M&A's. Central aspects of an analysis are to identify cultural problems and to identify key elements which determine the M&A process. Based on this analysis the goal of this thesis is
to develop a basic cultural integration toolkit that could solve the identified cultural problems. This toolkit could be used in all kinds of M&A's, working like a structured mind map. Executives, key personnel, and other in integration work involved people would benefit from a solid guidance through an integration process.

1.3 Research Method

The complexity of this topic in conjunction with the goal of developing a basic M&A toolkit led to applying an inductive approach. Consequently, this paper is based exclusively on secondary data. Although expert interviews from own M&A experiences would underline certain issues this paper seeks to cover a broader range.

Research has shown that there is a great selection of case studies and models supporting M&A integration available. These include single case studies oriented on specific transactions within the same sector, or country, or supporting cross-border transactions, mergers of equals but also models combined with case study elements referring to special integration stages. There are also models for specific business strategies available.

This paper's data collection is based on sources, which were published between 1996 and 2012. The majority of sources are not older than seven years. The collected data include secondary meeting minutes, recently published articles, books, academic documents, studies, and consultancy reports. All of them refer to integration topics and a variety of M&A aspects providing an overview or deeper insight in these topics. As such, they serve the purpose of this paper.

1.4 Structure

Section 2 starts with definitions and further delimitations. Section 3 shows the impact of M&A's in general and during the M&A stages. This chapter finishes with the identification of cultural problems and key drivers in the M&A process. Section 4 introduces various integration models. Prior to this the analysis approach is outlined. The model introduction finishes with comparing and evaluating them. Section 5 develops a basic cultural integration toolkit. The paper ends in section 6 with a short review and provides an outlook on future developments and research areas.

2 Definitions

The correlation between M&A's and culture issues is considered as a framework for this study. Before discussing them more in detail, relating key elements will be defined in this chapter. Section 2.1 starts with basic hard issues such as transactions and due diligence. The soft issues culture and culture clash will be explained in section 2.2. The chapter finishes with clarifying trust and language as crucial parts within this framework.

2.1 Transactions and Due Diligence

There are several definitions of "Mergers" and "Acquisitions". This paper refers to Trompenaar's clear definitions:

> "Mergers entail two organizations integrating into a third entity. [...] An acquisition is when one company buys another and integrates it into its own organization. [...] A strategic partnership or alliance may differ in this regard as there may only be integration of a department or a smaller part of an organization." (Trompenaars, 2010, p. 4)

Due to their various impacts on culture clashes M&A's are further divided into *"mergers of equals"*, and *"mergers of un-equals"*, as well as *"acquisitions and integration"*, and *"acquisitions and separation"* (Schuler, 2001, p. 240).
Looking at M&A's by direction does not correlate with culture issues and is therefore not part of this paper.
Conducting M&A's happens in stages. A description of typical M&A stages includes: 1) a pre-combination stage, 2) the combination or integration stage, and 3) the solidification or assessment stage (Schuler, 2001, p. 243). Merger stages will be discussed further in chapter four during the introduction and development of integration models.
The pre-combination stage includes the performance of due diligence, which is defined by Achtleitner as:

> "careful examination and analysis of a company, especially in view of its economic, legal, tax and financial situation, which is made by a prospective purchaser of a business" (see Gabler Wirtschafts-lexikon Online, translation by the author).

Even though *"due diligence has only limited ability to set accurate expectations of total synergies"* (McLetchie, 2010, p. 11), it is a vital process in deal making. Due diligence covers all business areas: finance including, commerce, legal, operation, strategy, IT, HR and culture. Figure 2.1 shows due diligence types by frequency of conduction. The graphic indicates clearly that HR due diligence was only performed in rare cases although it is one of the first process steps of cultural due diligence.

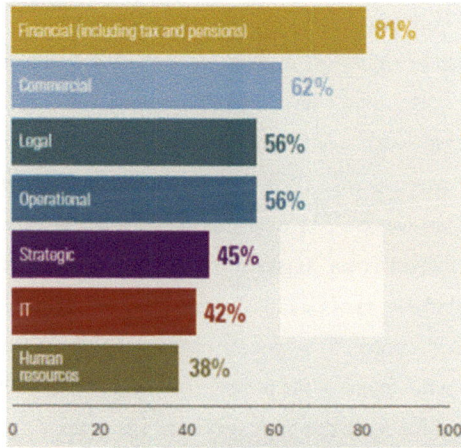

Figure 2. Due Diligence Types
(Source: KPMG, 2011, p. 18)

According to Carleton culture due diligence (CDD) is "a diagnostic process conducted to ascertain the degree of cultural alignment or compatibility between companies" (Carleton, 2004, p. 53).

2.2 Culture and Culture Clashes

Research of general culture definitions resulted in two definitions, which seem to cover the broadest spectrum. Schein defines culture as:

> "pattern of basic assumptions – invented, discovered, or developed, by a given group as it learns to cope with its problems of external adaptation and internal integration – that has worked well enough to be considered valid, and, therefore, to be taught to new members as the correct way to perceive, think and feel in relation to those problems" (Schein, 2004, p. 17).

Hofstede summarizes culture as:

> "the collective programming of the mind that distinguishes the members of one group or category of people from another" (Hofstede, 2001, p. 9).

Company culture is expressed in behavior of people who have their own culture, which is composed of elements reflecting their origins. Hofstede's fundamental definition refers to nations. He gives solid examples of how national cultures affect company culture. Therefore, his definition is used as a starting point in this paper. Consequently, this paragraph focuses on Hofstede's IBM study, represented in Hofstede, 2001, in order to understand the complexity of culture. Although the IBM study takes only a small part of the today's business world into account its findings provide the most comprehensive overview about culture and a basis for other academic work. Therefore, other opinions are not considered in this definition section. Culture consists of values expressed in symbols, heroes and rituals - in total: behavior. Hofstede sliced culture into impact levels: family, school, work, politics, religion, society. This paper refers to level 'work' exclusively. In a second step Hofstede divided culture into five basic issues: 1) Power Distance (PD) referring to power distribution between boss and staff, 2) Uncertainty Avoidance (UA) referring to the stress level which occurs about an unknown future, 3) Individualism versus Collectivism (IDV) reflecting the orientation towards groups or individuals, 4) Masculinity versus Femininity (MAS) referring to emotional roles between men and women, 5) long-term versus short-term orientation (LTO) referring to the people's focus on the future or the present (Hofstede, 2001, p. 29). Figure 2.2 outlines three examples of key differences per basic problem. The index columns "low" and "high" show indicators for the specific basic problem. For instance: a low power distance index for basic problem "Power Distance" can be identified when a) the company is decentralized structured and has a flat hierarchy, b) the leadership style is rather consultative, c) the staff expect to be consulted before decisions about their work will be made.

Cultural Key Differences in Work Situations			
Basic Problem	Key Differences	Index	
		Low	High
Power Distance	structure / hierarchy	decentralized / flat	centralized / tall
	leadership style	consultative	authoritative
	staff espect	to be consulted	to be told
Uncertainty Avoindance	loyalty to employer	weak	strong
	power depends on	position and relationships	control of uncertainties
	orientation	relationship	task
Collectivism versus Individualism	managment of	groups	individuals
	orientation	relationship	task
	staff commitment	low	high
Masculinity versus Femininity	managers expected to	use intuition, deal with feelings, and seek consensus	be decisive, firm, assertive, agressive, competitive
	resolution of conflicts through	problem solving, compromise, negotiation	denying them or fighting until the best "man" wins
	job stress	lower	higher
Long- versus Short-Term Orientation	focus on	short term results / bottom line	building relationships & market position
	confidence	probabilistic	either full or none
	way of thinking	analytic	synthetic

Figure 3. Key Differences by Basic Culture Problem
(Source: Hofstede, 2001)

The next figure illustrates different types of indices for selected countries. The LTO index is excluded due to the lack of source data.

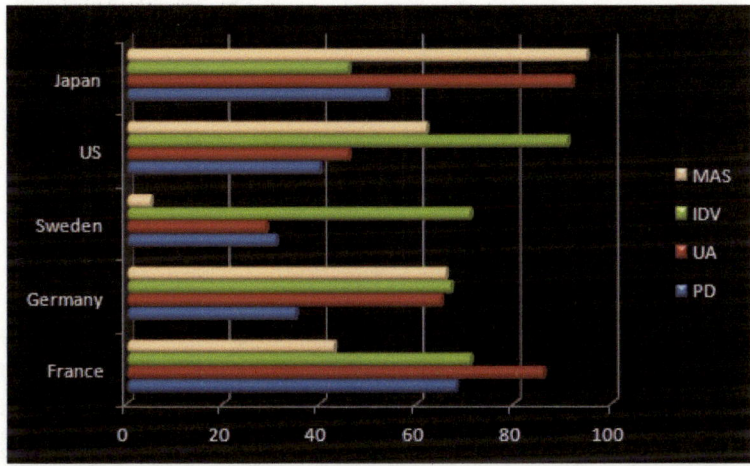

Figure 4. Culture Problem Indices by Country
(Source: Hofstede, 2001)

Germany, France, and Sweden were selected as examples representing differences between western oriented European countries in contrast with the US and Japan. France shows a high power distance index, indicating people are used to tall hierarchy and authority. On the contrary, Germany has a much lower PD index. Hierarchy is rather flat and the leadership style fairly consultative. A combination of companies based in Germany and in France could cause great misunderstandings leading further to decreasing productivity for instance. See all available data in Appx. A.

The next basic soft fact is culture clash. Carleton defines culture clash as differences between in M&A involved companies about beliefs, importance, values, measurements, and treatment of people, decision making, managing and supervising, and communicating (Carleton, 2004, p. 13). Culture clash folds an organization and its way of doing business into another organization (ibid).

2.3 Trust and Language

Chapter two finishes with looking at two crucial culture components.

The first one is trust, which is seen *"as a fundamental pillar of human integration"* (Trompenaars, 2010, p. xiv). Covey defines trust as:

> "function of [...] character and competence. Character includes your integrity, your motive your intent with people. Competence includes your capabilities, your skills, your results, your track record. [...] Ethics [...] is foundational to trust but itself insufficient (Covey, 2010, p. 30).

Covey stresses a direct connection between trust and a company's performance as follows:

> "When trust goes down, speed will also go down and costs will go up. [...] When trust goes up, speed will also go up and costs will go down." (Covey, 2010, p. 13).

The second component is language. A basic problem with language is that people may hold different expectations about the use of language (Hofstede, 2001, p. 21). Expressing oneself in another language means automatically adopting a certain frame of references and a limitation of vocabulary (Hofstede, 2001, p. 424). Monolingual native speakers tend to assume what a foreign speaker can express in the native speaker's language is all that the foreigner has on his mind (ibid).

3 Impact of M&A's

After defining the framework for M&A correlations in the previous chapter, this chapter highlights M&A consequences. These impacts on organizations have direct impact on their culture and vise versa because culture is embedded within the organization (Carleton, 2004, p. 32). Sample impacts will be presented referring to M&A stages and outlining cultural problems. Key elements, which are needed to solve these problems, will then be derived.

3.1 In General

The following example is based on a study by marketline, 2011. The second largest player in the pharmacy industry with an M&A history back to 1800 acquires companies around the world. Still, the company had faced a failure in its R&D pipeline after the last merger. In contrast to that they started an operational program which has compensated this shortcoming largely and led to market growth of 15% outside the US and Europe. This example reflects direct impacts of M&A's on performance but it also proves the company's M&A strategy, which obviously had cultural problems mitigated if not eliminated. Furthermore an M&A success role is more essential in deal making then size and frequency of deals (Cottin, 2011, p. 1 and Rehm, 2012, p. 5).

When two companies are involved in a merger or acquisition one overall dilemma occurs: culture clash – the meeting of organizational and national culture at both sides. This leads to culture integration problems in most cases.

3.2 During the M&A Stages

This section focuses on the M&A impacts during the transaction stages. The pre-merger phase includes among others negotiations (Schneck, 2007, p. 11 and Faber, 2007, p. 12). Disrespecting nature of control and decision making structure on either side, or ignoring the distribution of decision making power among people, or not tolerating emotional needs of negotiators may lead to breaking off the negotiations (Hofstede, 2001, p. 435) and probably causing total loss of the deal. Cultural problems are clearly expressed in misunderstanding and lack of intercultural competence.

Conducting due diligence is another part of the pre-merger phase. Several studies suggest that acquirers admitted a desire for a better due diligence and planning, a faster integration and more attention to HR and cultural issues – the next time (KPMG, 2011, p. 19 and Knechtel, 2009, p. 12). Connections between individual due diligence areas cannot be explored since they are conducted separately from each other (Knechtel, 2009, p. 12). Consequently, creating of values and synergies is rather inefficient and will not improve the new company's performance. This impact of missing an integration strategy and plan results in integration issues.

Those companies that prioritized the selection of the management team during the pre-deal planning stage were 26% more likely to have a successful deal (KPMG, 1999, p. 16). The lack of a selected management or integration team would slow down the integration process and create an integration problem.

The next samples overlap from the merger to the post-merger phase.

People who are involved in an M&A transaction face changes of organizational structure, roles, in working processes and tools, maybe relocation and many more. They feel losses leading to increased uncertainty and anxiety concerning their future (Cartwright, 1996, pp. 48-49). Preoccupation increases in those affected, eventually resulting in loss of productivity. A study about culture shock indicates that a more than 15% of effectiveness is lost because of worry, rumors, and misinformation (Gitelson, 2001, p. 41). Losing effectiveness due to lack of integrating people indicates integration issues as cultural problem.

Referring to Cartwright, 1996, pp. 39-40, affected people often live through loss in stages. Stage 1 points out extreme shock expressed in disbelief and denial. Stage 2 shows anger through rage and resentment followed in stage 3 by emotional bargaining through uncertainty about individual job future, resulting in depression. Finally acceptance takes place in stage 4, indicating that the past is gone forever. Because of these impacts on staff M&A's frequently result in loss. Loss of talent due to role duplicity or due to resignations including executives indicates again an integration issue (Cartwright, 1996, p. 45-46 and Krug, 2003 p. 14).

The resignation of executives decreases the leadership stability and disrupts communication lines. Krug's investigations show that if a company is not able *"to keep the critical mass of the old guard [...] a domino effect"* will be recognized *"at least nine years out"* – and perhaps much longer (Krug, 2003, p. 15). The cultural problem is evidently lost talent.

Integration work is essential, its cost and duration is often underestimated (Knechtel, 2009, p. 8). Poor integration work deteriorates customer satisfaction and lead eventually to sales decline. Furthermore, the adaption of existing structure is often neglected. Therefore change management and integration work are seen as great challenges in M&A transactions. Cartwright suggests that integration takes between 3 and 5 years, in case of cross-border transactions even longer (Cartwright, 1996, p. 29).

Insufficient integration work would lead to "winning the battle while losing the war" (Carleton, 2004, p. 29), meaning the organization would lose much effectiveness. For instance, when processes in single departments are re-engineered they nevertheless have impact on other organizational components – which should be but often is not taken into account.

Another cultural problem is communication. Fight for control, rumors among staff and poor willingness to adopt the other culture are impacts, which often occur during M&As.

Differences in language may cause distance and isolation due to the lack of language skills at various staff levels (Piekkari, 2005, p. 334). Sometimes experts are prevented from actively attending meetings when they are not able to express themselves properly in the new company language (Piekkari, 2005, p. 337). Limited language skills lead to limited acceptance among colleagues, which complicates business live of those affected. This example shows a communication problem.

3.3 Cultural Problems and Key Drivers in M&A Stages

The discussion about impacts of M&A's has identified following cultural problems: (1) lack of cultural integration, (2) lack of intercultural competence, (3) lost talent, (4) misunderstandings, and (5) communication problems. Integration models should solve these problems. Knowing the problems raises the question of which elements need to be included in the M&A process to avoid those problems. The lack of cultural integration could be mitigated by a clear **integration strategy** and a detailed **integration plan**. The lack of intercultural competences should be eliminated by **cross-cultural training sessions** building up knowledge, awareness, understanding and providing guidance through case studies and simulations. Losing talent and communication problems should be avoided by a clear **communication strategy** and **communication process**. Misunderstandings should be completely avoided through a combination of the introduced key elements. Conducting a **cultural due diligence** is also seen as a key element, as so as the use of **integration teams**, and **post merger monitoring**. A **systemic approach** should be added as last important key element.

4 Integration Models as Solution Alternatives

After learning about M&A impacts in the previous chapter two questions arise: 1) how can the identified cultural problems be solved within the entire M&A process? 2) How can the detected key elements be implemented? This chapter seeks answers in existing integration models. It starts with laying out the research approach. Selected models will be introduced afterwards and evaluated with respect to answering the two questions.

4.1 Analysis Approach

The data sources were systematically screened and summarized. Evaluating the source data started with a rough definition of target categories. Books have been summarized with focus on these categorized topics. In search for contributions to the main topics data and statistics have been further categorized into subtopics by category and have been coded accordingly. Coded data has then been analyzed in closer search for relevance leading to findings which are expressed in this paper. Statistics from a specific source have been consolidated to deliver the basis for statistical examples and graphs. Existing integration models have been distinguished between more general and supplemental meanings. Interpretations of these models will be presented in this chapter.

4.2 Selection of Existing Integration Models

4.2.1 The Delta Model by Faber

(Faber, 2007, pp. 16-46)

Faber's model (see Appx B) covers the classical three M&A phases (pre-merger, merger, post-merger). He adopted the delta model by Hax for his work which he based mostly on his own experiences and to some extent on secondary data. Faber emphasizes on flexible entries, which make this model applicable for each involved individual regardless of the M&A phase. The entry points are explained as follows.

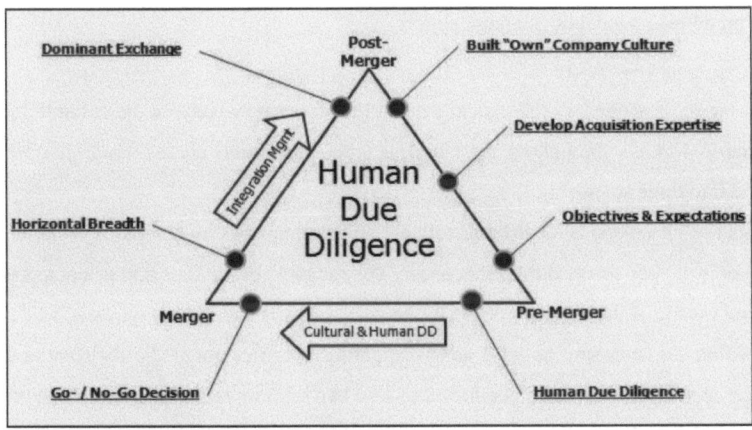

Figure 5. Human Due Diligence Delta Model
(Source: Faber, 2007, p. 41 – simplified by the author)

Faber begins with "building the own company culture". Key transactions at this stage are seen as development of a long-term strategy and a cultural integration strategy. Educating and training employees, giving HR people key roles in all acquisition phases and a selection of acquisitions to learn from contribute to the step "develop acquisition expertise". Faber emphasizes that senior managers need to agree on "objectives and expectations" for each deal and communicate them. It is important to decide on the depth of integration between cultural blending, takeover, and pluralism. The goal of the "Human Due Diligence" step is to understand the target's culture, people, size and volume of the customer base, geographical presence, and product portfolio. Faber suggests to start human due diligence at the same time as the other parts of the due diligence. The outcome of the human due diligence is summarized in step "Go- / No-Go Decision". If the findings prove that the cultural differences are too large and there is no willingness to change on either side further negotiations may be cancelled and consequently the long term strategy may be revised. If the findings prove the contrary integration levels and activities, creating a task force and identifying the best processes are seen as final key transactions at this stage. After the deal is signed integration management starts covering the "Horizontal Breadth". Faber stresses the importance of communication, culture adoptions, using best practices, technology, talent, systems. The final stage focuses on keeping the new momentum.

4.2.2 The Three Phase Model by Wollersheim

(Wollersheim, 2008, pp. 29-31)

This model is based on secondary theoretical data and focuses exclusively on the cultural due diligence piece in M&A's throughout the classical three transaction phases. Each phase is further divided into three steps.

The overall goal of phase one is identifying suitable target companies by comparing cultures. Mitigating risks is the key driver during this phase. The outcome of the first step is a comprehensive cultural profile of the own company. Wollersheim suggests to look at symbols, values and beliefs within the company as well as investigating specifics about the own national culture. The same analysis should be conducted in step two with respect of the target company. Step three finishes the first phase by comparing the culture profiles and identifying a target company. Goal of the second phase is the development of an integration strategy. Findings about culture will be analyzed more in detail so that specific cultural differences become visible. Evaluating these results is the basis for developing an integration strategy, which will be realized in phase three. Both cultures eventually "meet" in the implementation phase three. These cultural clashes will be managed by rolling out the integration strategy. The last phase finishes with success control and alteration of the strategy for an even better fit.

4.2.3 The Three Phase Model by Schneck

(Schneck, 2007, pp. 7-12)

Schneck recommends staying focused on CDD during the entire M&A transaction as so as with all other due diligence pieces. His model is based on primary and secondary data and contains three stages as well.

The first stage in Schneck's model concentrates on data collection and analysis in parallel with the planning of the transaction. Based on a rough content- and document analysis he suggests a comparison of cultures, indentifying key differences and risk areas. As additional data become available during the pre-merger and negotiation phase, further analyses and observations take place in stage two. Schneck highlights the use of further instrumentations such as single and group interviews with key personnel, along with simulations and questionnaires. Evaluating all data leads to cultural profiles visualizing culture fits and clashes. The goal of stage three is the cultural integration. Milestones help to achieve this goal. They include defining company coals, vision and mission statement and an integration strategy. Responsible integration teams will be created to develop and implement integration programs and communication models. The third stage finishes with success control of the entire program.

4.2.4 The Three Phase Model by Schuler

(Schuler, 2001, pp. 7-12)

This model (see Appx. C) is based on secondary data and reflects parallels to the previous three models as it again focuses along the three classical transaction stages and on HR issues in particular. Schuler provides both insight about correlations and guidance broken out by M&A stage. On top of that he expresses the role of an integration manager and characteristics of successful business leaders completing his overview.

Schuler starts in the pre-combination stage with identifying the reasons for the transaction and appointing an M&A team and leader. In a next step potential targets will be identified. After that, both managing the transaction and the learning from it will be planned. Schuler sees the selection of an integration manager as crucial point for conducting the change process. The integration manager makes decisions about staff, the new culture, structure and policies. A communication process will be laid out and followed rather frequently. In the last stage the announcement of the new leadership and staffing will be made. In addition to that, the new organization as a whole in terms of strategies and structures, stakeholder's concerns and culture will be assessed. Depending on the outcome of the assessments, certain aspects will be revised if needed. The last piece in this stage covers learning from the M&A process.

4.2.5 The Organizational Fit by Cartwright

(Cartwright, 1996)

Cartwright's model, which is based on experience and secondary data, concentrates on her own "culture" definitions. In addition to that she distinguishes three integration possibilities in conjunction with this model. Hereby is the degree of constraint placed on an individual used as measurement. Overall Cartwright considers the degree of similarity between combining organizations as crucial success factor.

Since this paper does not seek instruction for specific merger types, both the specific culture definition and a discussion of the three merger types shall not be examined further.

Cartwright's integration work is divided into M&A stages. The pre-combination stage covers preplanning tasks, such as knowing the own culture, research target company, consult with personnel functions, arrive with an agenda of people issues and areas for discussion. An initial assessment of the target culture should be conducted during this stage, contract terms should be outlined. The next stage concerns the legal announcement. Employees should be introduced to the new organization. Along with that, future change and integration should be explained. In order to achieve these goals a communication strategy and plan including a feedback mechanism need to be prepared. The next stage relates to the "honeymoon phase" which reflects the cultural change. The goal is to understand both cultures, unfreeze the existing culture, and accelerate the change process. Cartwright suggests following procedures: informal discussions and observations, creating joint working parties and inter-organizational team buildings, conducting an employee survey, use various culture change approaches. The final stage concerns monitoring M&A success. Essential elements in this stage entail recognizing early warnings, dealing with employees stress, keeping in touch throughout all hierarchical levels. In order to learn from this transaction an integration program should be put together.

4.2.6 The Customized CDD Model by Carleton

(Carleton, 2004)

Carleton is co-founder and CEO of Vector Group. His model is based on experience and secondary data. He indicates CDD *"should be viewed as mandatory step"* (Carleton, 2004, p. 53). His model is directed along the M&A stages as well.

Carleton uses the organizational scan model (see Appx D) for assessing the company culture. This scan follows a systemic approach. It is an organizational view on external & internal factors in conjunction with conditions, processes, and outputs. Carleton suggests using this tool rather periodic and not during M&A's exclusively.

Further major steps in his CDD model are: assessment and detailed cultural assessment of the target, alignment and integration planning. Carleton's customized CCD model differs from the traditional CDD models in one aspect. Instead of describing all cultural elements of an organization this model is rather based on functional culture. That way it provides flexibility and a systemic approach. Carleton achieves this flexibility by grouping the CDD findings within twelve domains.

Figure 4.2 shows CDD tasks per M&A stage in a simplified format. It reflects the point in time at which each task starts but excludes circles to keep the graph at an overview level. The first step is the integration of the executive group and contains the implementation of time sensitive issues as well as issues-based team building sessions. In a next step all managers will be involved. "Tiger Team" will be built to solve a specific problem within a short time frame exclusively. A multi-rater 360-degree feedback system will be put in place and follow up sessions will be hold. After that all staff sessions will be conducted to align the total organization finishing with follow-up and re-engineering sessions and continuing success measurement.

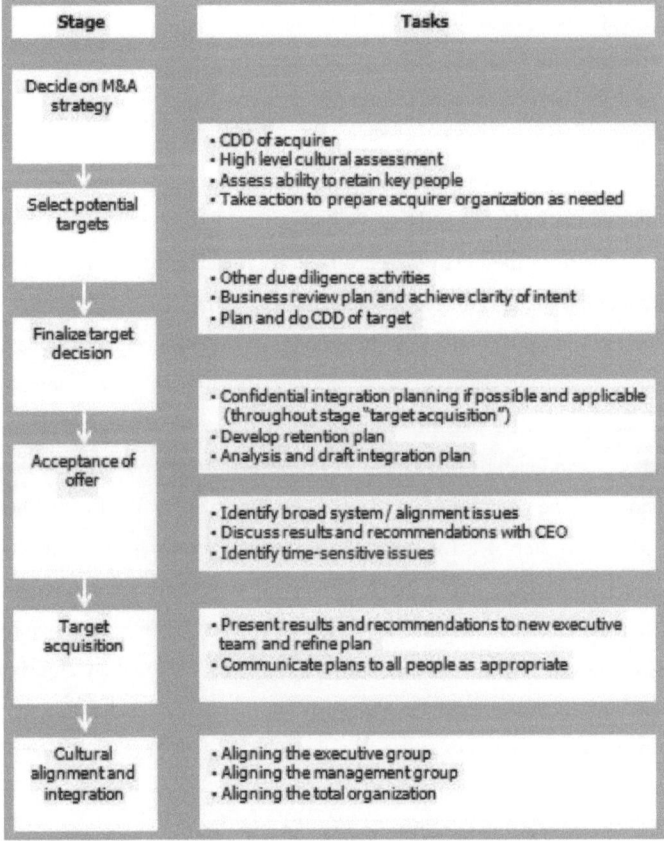

Figure 6. Cultural Due Diligence Assessment
(Source: Carleton, 2004, p. 3 – simplified by the author)

Various checklists, surveys and interview sheets, which support the entire process, are available for group sessions and education in Carleton's publications and can be requested at Vector Groups website.

4.2.7 The Three Phase Framework by Trompenaars

(Trompenaars, 2010)

This ten-step-model is divided in three main phases. Dilemma thinking is used as reconciliation process. This approach generates integrated value based on the strengths both parties contribute. Indicators to the classical M&A stages are not given although the model is designed to be used in M&A transactions. Underlying data include mostly experiences but also secondary data.

In the first phase a compelling business case will be created. It starts with step 1) re/defining vision and mission in order to integrate the new organization. Assessing business challenges through business dilemmas is the next procedure in step 2) leading to a clarified new challenge. Core values and key purpose for the new integrated organization will be defined in step 3) by assessments of purposes and values. Tompenaars uses the organizational value profiler (OVP) – see Appx. E, and the personal value profiler (PVP) based on his definitions of culture elements and conducted interviews. Both tools diagnose the different corporate cultures as well as the relationships that employees have with their organization. After that values and behaviors will be chosen to facilitate linking the values with effective behavior. This procedure comprises step 4). The first phase finishes with step 5) compelling the business case for the integration. The goal of the second phase is the development of an implementation strategy, its objectives and KPI's. Key drivers will be defined in step 6). They serve the purpose of customizing the communication design, the methodology and content of the cultural integration process and provide managers with feedback for coaching purposes. Step 7) continues with developing the integration strategy through clear objectives and KPI's. The last phase aims at developing a systemic alignment and value awareness starting with the systemic alignment in step 8). Values will be connected with visions and mission in several workshops. Conducting value and awareness programs in a blended learning approach is included in step 9) in order to raise awareness in larger organizations. The final step 10) contains continuing re-evaluation by monitoring and controlling changes.

References to various tools are given and extracts of various tools are provided for a better understanding and more transparency.

4.2.8 Various Supplemental Models and Studies

As supplemental models and studies are those considered which refer to M&A types or specific M&A aspects.

This paragraph refers to Drori, 2011. He has developed a model for merger of equals of high tech start-up companies. Drori recommends adopting a *"flexible approach to align equality with strategic and operational needs"* (Drori, 2011, p. 633). His conclusion indicates that a shared understanding of the common business environment led to the merger of equal type. This type was considered to succeed in a new market. Drori outlines a major dilemma during post merger integration caused by internal competition.

The next part refers to a model by Zhu, 2007. It stresses a four step integration procedure of cross-border M&A's. Zhu recognizes respecting and understanding the culture of others, and communication as basic management principles. Zhu stated: *"People are core of cross-cultural management"* (Zhu, 2007, p. 42). The four stages cover localization strategy, meaning the new company strategy should consider local condition. Changing the target culture to the culture of the acquirer is considered as next stage followed by integration work. The last stage includes third party support in case of huge cultural gaps. Culture clashes can be mitigated through applying the described systematic procedure. This example reflects integration issues and lack of intercultural competence as cultural problems.

Focusing now on Deloitte's post merger integration study by Gerds, 2010, which refers specifically to monitor post merger risks. Findings were condensed to four post merger integration risks: synergy, structure, project, and people and further divided in two to three elements per risk. Gerds recommends completing his survey to asses post merger integration chances. He sees poor integration planning and lack of success control by integration stages as need for developing his tool.

The last part in this section refers to Engert 2010. This McKinsey model captures value as soon as the deal is announced within six steps. This comprehensive guide stresses the importance of integration planning and management.

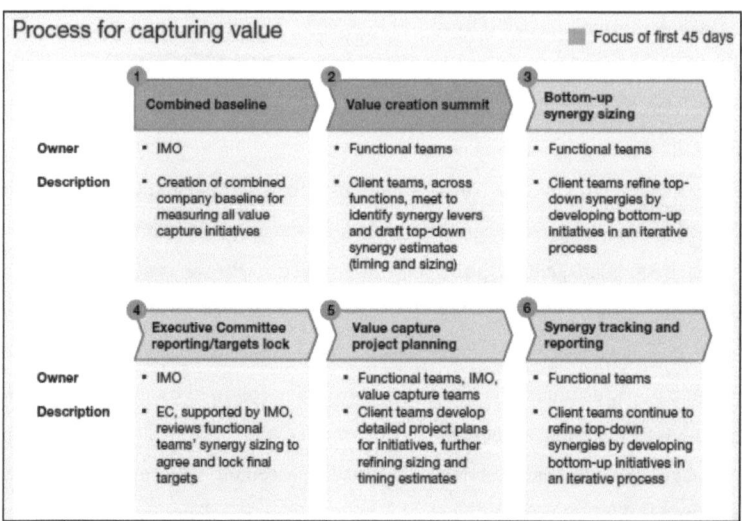

Figure 7. Process for Capturing Value
(Source: Engert, 2010, p. 25)

4.3 Evaluation of the Models

All models and studies provide great insight in various aspects and steps of M&A transactions. Figure 4.4 shows a comparison of the key elements per discussed model.

All models develop a strategy and an integration strategy based on a data collection. Wollersheim had not included the development of a communication strategy in her model Her summary can been seen as a high level basis model to derive an integration model and customize it for own needs. Even though Trompenaars had not specifically mentioned the term "cross-cultural training", still his dilemma approach serves the same effect. Faber's model refers at a very early stage to educate the staff whereas all other models do not mention cross-cultural trainings at all. This result is surprising and shows a weak point because people in international roles need to be at least bilingual and need to understand the culture of their counterparts. On the other hand, workshops and result analysis are mentioned in each model. Conducting these tasks may include some sort of training as well.

Comparison of Existing Models	Faber	Woltersheim	Schneck	Schuler	Cartwright	Carleton	Trompenaars
Strategy	✓	✓	✓	✓	✓	✓	✓
Integration strategy	✓	✓	✓	✓	✓	✓	✓
Cross-cultural training	trainings						✓
Communication strategy	✓		✓	✓	✓	✓	✓
CDD	✓	✓	✓	✓	✓	customized CDD	✓
Integration teams	✓			✓		✓	
Post merger monitoring	✓	✓	✓	✓	✓	✓	✓
Limitation to M&A		to CDD	to CDD	to HR issues			
Coverage of all M&A stages	✓	✓	✓	✓	✓	✓	indirect
Systemic Approach						✓	semi
Instruments provided			examples are only named	interview sheet	culture assessment	various for all stages	references provided
Underlying theories	experience & secondary data	secondary data	primary & secondary data	secondary data	experience & secondary data	experience & secondary data	experience & secondary data

Figure 8. Comparison of Existing Integration Models

Cultural due diligence plays an important role in all models. They strongly recommend conducting CDD in parallel with the other due diligence pieces. Carleton provides an even more sophisticated approach referring to a customized CDD. The importance of integration teams has not been mentioned very often. Still Schneck's, Cartwrights, Carelton's and Trompenaars' models stress instruments such as interview sheets, surveys and simulations. Consequently people use these instruments. The models just do not point out to integration teams specifically. Generally, integration team work could be used in expatriate situations as well. They could help the expatriate to be prepared for the international assignment as well as at the point in time of his return. Post merger monitoring and success control is included in every model. A few express summarizing a business case and sharing it as "best practice" solution for the next transaction. The grid shows that some of the models are specifically designed for CDD and HR issues. Such focus is a solution option. Yet it could create danger of losing the overview and missing the impacts on other organizational components, more according to "winning the battle while losing the war" (Carleton, 2004, p. 29) as described in section 4.2.8. Interfaces to other organizational components or M&A transactions would have helped to understand the meaning better. The systemic by Carleton and to some extent by Trompenaars' is seen as necessity for sustainability and long-term success of the transaction. What seem missing are instruments to conduct each single step, such as interview sheets, checklists, surveys. Overall guidance is provided in each model, ready for execution and / or adaption. Still the "How exactly" is hardly answered in any of these models. Only Carleton provides a set of instruments for the steps in his model. The information about the underlying theories shows that all models are based on solid ground. The high level model by Wollersheim is considered too theoretical. A practical reference would help orienting and understanding the steps even better and would indicate room for own customization. The supplemental models and studies confirm the identified problems. They express the need for considering a selection of the key elements according to their aspects. The overall comparison clearly indicates that none of the models include all defined key elements and characteristics. Nevertheless, the models can be used to solve cultural problems. This paper seeks to fulfill both requirements: solving cultural problems and including all key elements - in the next chapter.

5 A Set of Cultural Integration Tools

After evaluating a selection of existing integration models with respect to the identified cultural problems and key drivers, a cultural integration toolkit will be developed. The lack of a comprehensive set of tools, which integrates all key elements and provides detailed guidance and instruments, is the gap this toolkit should fill.

Each entity is unique in its company culture. This uniqueness creates one similarity between all M&A transactions: every involved entity faces culture clash created by M&A transactions. This is inevitable and happens regardless of any point of view. Culture clashes can be found even in transactions where both entities are based in the same country and placed within the same industry sector. Therefore this toolkit is seen as a general integration model. The provided instruments can be used immediately, or be adopted, or not used if not needed – depending on the M&A transaction.

The model shows the classical transaction stages and indicates the identified key drivers for each stage. Some key drivers overlap, therefore they are shown multiple times. The model outlines necessary steps integrating the specific key element. It recommends sample instruments which could be used fulfilling this step. "Supplementary Help" offers additional instruments in case they are needed.

The model starts in the pre-transaction phase with defining the long-term strategy. The strategy should be assessed by using known portfolio techniques. After that, an integration strategy should be derived. It is recommended to use the introduced organizational scan in order to get the full picture about the own company. A sample scan is included in Appx. D. Publications from Carleton provide an organizational scan survey that can be used for own group sessions.

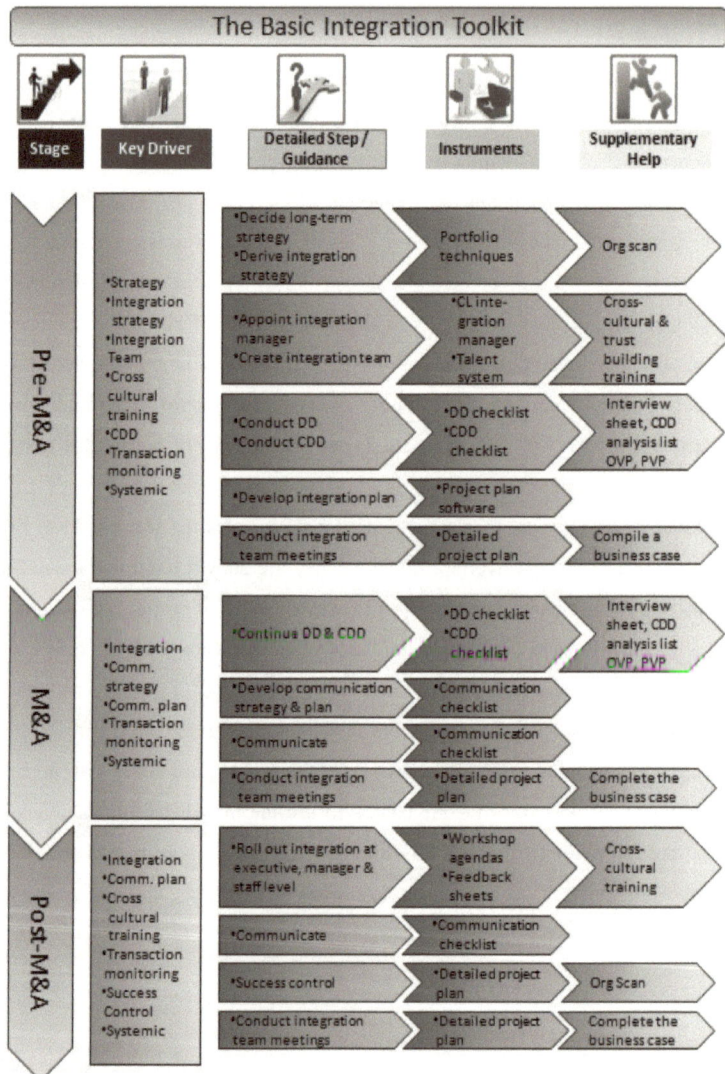

Figure 9. The Cultural Integration Toolkit

This toolkit continues with appointing an integration manager. This step is crucial for the following processes. The integration manager should create the new structure and speed up the entire integration. He is also in charge of all soft issues. Specifics of an integration manager profile and tasks are provided in Appx F. Once the integration manager is appointed the integration team should be selected from the company's own talent system. Both the entire team and the integration manager should bring intercultural competences and trust building abilities with them to be able to fulfill future integration tasks. If their skill sets exclude these features they should attend a cross-cultural training and improve their trust building skills. Sample contents of an intercultural training are provided in Appx G. A trust building checklist is included in Appx H. As the integration team is now prepared, it develops an integration plan considering impacts on all departments to follow the systemic approach. Project plan software helps defining milestones, tasks, allocating resources and reflecting timelines. It is strongly recommended to continue in a project manner. This way transaction monitoring and systemic alignment takes place frequently. Based on the strategies and the project plan a business case should be composed and further completed during the transaction. The business case helps keeping the strategic focus and serves as best practice case for future transactions. In parallel with the project plan the due diligence pieces start and the organizational scan results are further analyzed with respect to CDD. Due diligence and cultural due diligence checklists along with interview sheets are recommended as instruments. Samples are available in Carleton's publications. Organizational and personal value profilers can also be used. A sample is shown in Appx. E.

The due diligences are further conducted during the transaction phase including interviews with key people and HR – among others. Organizational and cultural profiles of the target company are composed by using the same instruments as mentioned above. It is also recommended that the integration manager attends the negotiations in a consultancy role using his intercultural competence and tact. A communication strategy and a plan will be developed. A checklist about the when, where, who, how, and feedback channels serves as instrument of the announcement. It is crucial to communicate to all staff levels and externals the same messages during the transaction and post-transaction phase. This way risk of rumors will be mitigated and trust will be built. Team meetings and process control as well as completing the business case are integral parts in the merger and post-merger phase.

The integration roll out in the post-transaction phase should be organized top-down, from the executive level through the manager level to the staff level. Managers serve as role model and staff orients on these role models. The integration at each level is conducted in workshop-feedback-circles. This procedure provides information, reconciles dilemmas (see Appx I) which have been identified through the organizational scan, the OVP and the PVP. Cross cultural trainings should be extended to staff from the target organization to ease the process and future corporation. The last phase finishes with controlling post merger success and setting milestones for post transactional scans. The business case will finally be completed.

6 Conclusion

6.1 Summary and Conclusion

This study is focused on the development of an integration toolkit. The research aimed to identify two aspects: cultural problems which occur regardless of the merger and acquisition type and key drivers which determine the merger and acquisition process. Based on the results an integration toolkit should be developed. Secondary data were used in this study, compiled of books, academic work, and journals. Identified problems led to research for key drivers which need to be included in M&A transactions in order to avoid those identified problems. Research showed which of the key elements were implemented in existing integration models and that existing models could solve some of the problems.

Drawbacks of this approach are seen in various areas. Even though this study uses the inductive approach, moving from the details to the general, granularity levels and detail quantities have not been determined. More source data and greater granularity may have led to additional cultural problems and key drivers. The paper seeks to take this into consideration through the selection of introduced models. Still the results are not universal. Another downside could be established by the general approach. M&A transactions have been analyzed regardless of their type. Conducting the same analysis on transactions of the same type may have revealed other problems or greater shortcomings in the existing integration models. Also the selection of integration models is not universal. A limitation of research about M&A transactions for example within the EU could have revealed surprising results and questions, starting with the simple question: what is considered as a classical M&A transaction within the EU. EU companies already exist, e.g. EADS. What was considered as foreign subsidiary before becomes now a branch. – Is that considered to be an M&A transaction? Yet, the cultural impacts may not be different from what is discussed in this study.

Keeping such considerations in the background the source data for this thesis was selected carefully in order to gather a wide variety of data. The outlined results proved that awareness about culture clashes needs to be raised. M&A transactions become more and more difficult, as just briefly mentioned, and the integration processes speed up. This situation indicates a need for an integration model that includes all identified key elements.

In conclusion, the developed toolkit does cover all identified key elements and is able mitigate the identified cultural problems. "Managing culture clashes in M&A's" is possible with this developed toolkit. It could be accessed through network groups, integration groups and through classical publications as booklet, CD, e-book, and download.

6.2 Outlook and Recommendations

Increasing numbers of M&A transactions indicate that they become rather common. Even more surprising is that M&A's and their impacts can hardly be found in general management literature and studies. This topic should be equally included in general business administration studies, not as a digression but as a full booklet.

The cultural impact of M&A's on an organization is so tremendous that extensive CDD should become a mandatory requirement, also in order to protect shareholder value.

Future research areas could cover following aspects. How deal non-profit organizations with culture clash? They have different key drivers for mergers. Which approach do they use in their integration work? Could procedures be included in the basic integration tool?

Finally, one more research area could be: how does a culture clash affect individuals in a long run. Will the culture of an individual be changed over the years and will the changed individual culture brought back into the company? - The paper finishes with this outlook.

Appendices

Appendix A: PD, UA, MAS, IDV Indices by Country............................ VI
Appendix B: The Delta Model by Faber..VII
Appendix C: The Three Phase Model by Schuler................................ VIII
Appendix D: The Organizational Scan Model by Carleton IX
Appendix E: The Organizational Value Profiler....................................... X
Appendix F: Integration Manger Profile & Tasks XI
Appendix G: Cross-Cultural Training Content XII
Appendix H: Trust Building Checklist... XIII
Appendix I: Reconciling Dilemmas.. XIV

Appendix A

Power Distance (PD) / Uncertainty Avoidance (UA) / Individualism vs. Collectivism (IDV) / Masculinity vs. Femininity (MAS) Indices by Country

(Source: Hofstede, 200, pp. 87, 151, 215, 286)

	PDI	UAI	IDV	MAS
Malaysia	104	36	26	50
Guatemala	95	101	6	37
Panama	95	86	11	44
Philippines	94	44	32	64
Mexico	81	82	30	69
Venezuela	81	76	12	73
Arab countries	80	68	38	53
Ecuador	78	67	8	63
Indonesia	78	48	14	46
India	77	40	48	56
West Africa	77	54	20	46
Yugoslavia	76	88	27	21
Singapore	74	8	20	48
Brazil	69	76	38	49
France	68	86	71	43
Hong Kong	68	29	25	57
Colombia	67	80	13	64
Salvador	66	94	19	40
Turkey	66	85	37	45
Belgium	65	94	75	54
East Africa	64	52	27	41
Peru	64	87	16	42
Thailand	64	64	20	34
Chile	63	86	23	28
Portugal	63	104	27	31
Uruguay	61	100	36	38
Greece	60	112	35	57
South Korea	60	85	18	39
Iran	58	59	41	43
Taiwan	58	69	17	45
Spain	57	86	51	42
Pakistan	55	70	14	50
Japan	54	92	46	95
Italy	50	75	76	70
Argentina	49	86	46	56
South Africa	49	49	65	66
Jamaica	45	13	39	68
US	40	46	91	62
Canada	39	48	80	52
Netherlands	38	53	80	14
Australia	36	51	90	61
Costa Rica	35	86	15	21
Germany	35	65	67	66
UK	35	35	89	66
Switzerland	34	58	68	70
Finland	33	59	63	26
Norway	31	50	69	8
Sweden	31	29	71	5
Ireland	28	35	70	68
New Zealand	22	49	79	58
Denmark	18	23	74	16
Israel	13	81	54	47
Austria	11	70	55	79

Appendix B

The Delta Model – Cultural & Human Due Diligence – modified by the author
(Source: Faber, 2007, p. 41)

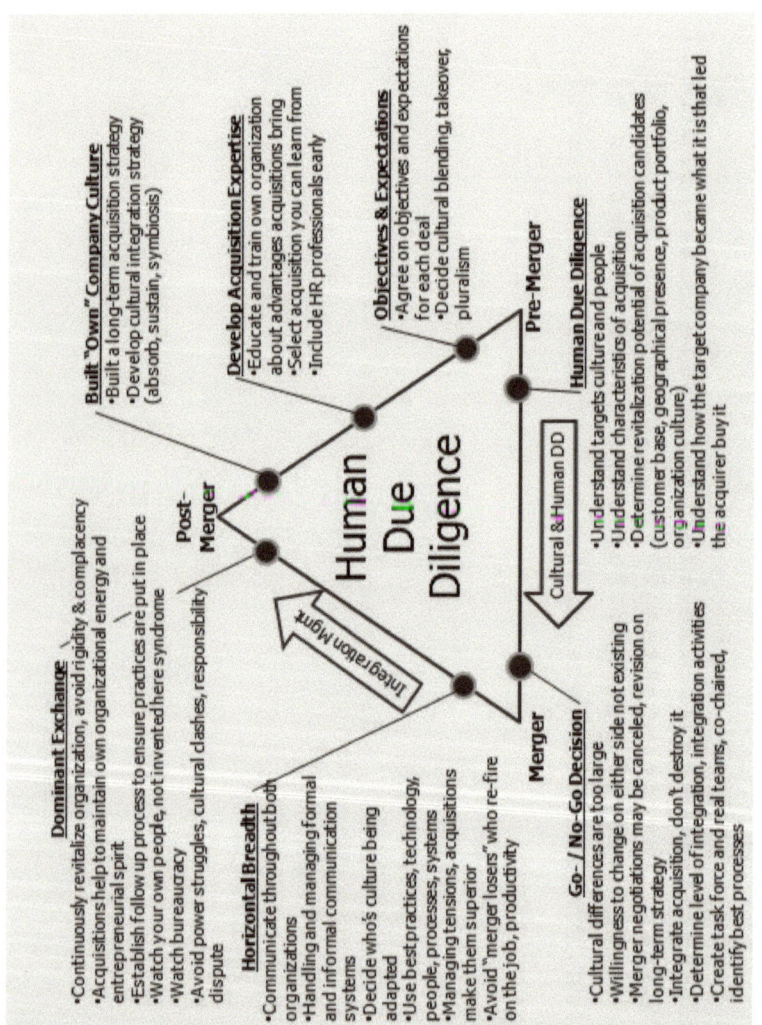

Appendix C

The Three Phase Model by Schuler

HR Issues	HR Implications and Actions
• Identifying reasons for the M & A • Forming M & A team/leader • Searching for potential partners • Selecting a partner • Planning for managing the process of the M and/or A • Planning to learn from the process	• Knowledge and understanding need to be disseminated • Leadership needs to be in place • Composition of team impacts success • Systematic and extensive pre-selection and selection are essential • Conducting thorough due diligence of all areas is vital • Cultural assessment • Planning for combination minimizes problems later • Creating practices for learning and knowledge transfer

Stage 1 – Pre-Combination (Source: Schuler, 2001, page 244)

HR Issues	HR Implications and Actions
• Selecting the integration manager • Designing/implementing teams • Creating the new structure/strategies/ leadership • Retaining key employees • Motivating the employees • Managing the change process • Communicating with and involving stakeholders • Deciding on the HR policies and practices	• Selecting the appropriate candidate • Creating team design and selection are critical for transition and combination success • Communicating is essential • Deciding on who stays and goes • Establishing a new culture, structure, and HR policies and practices is essential

Stage 2 – Combination – Integration of the Companies (Source: Schuler, 2001, page 244)

HR Issues	HR Implications and Actions
• Solidifying leadership and staffing • Assessing the new strategies and structures • Assessing the new culture • Assessing the new HR P & P • Assessing the concerns of stakeholders • Revising as needed • Learning from the process	• Elective leadership and staffing of the new entity are essential • Creating and evaluating a new structure • Melding two cultures needs assessment revision • The concerns of all stakeholders need to be addressed and satisfied • The new entity must learn

Stage 2 – Combination – Integration of the Companies (Source: Schuler, 2001, page 244)

Appendix D

The Organizational Scan Model by Carleton – modified by the author

(Source: Carleton, 2004, p. 40)

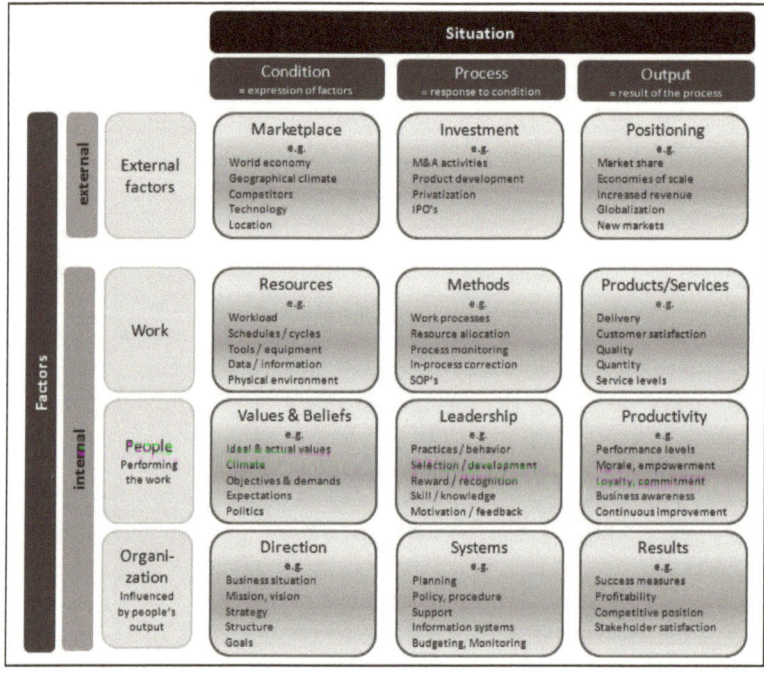

Appendix E

The Organizational Value Profiler by Trompenaars

(Source: Trompenaars, 2010, p.66)

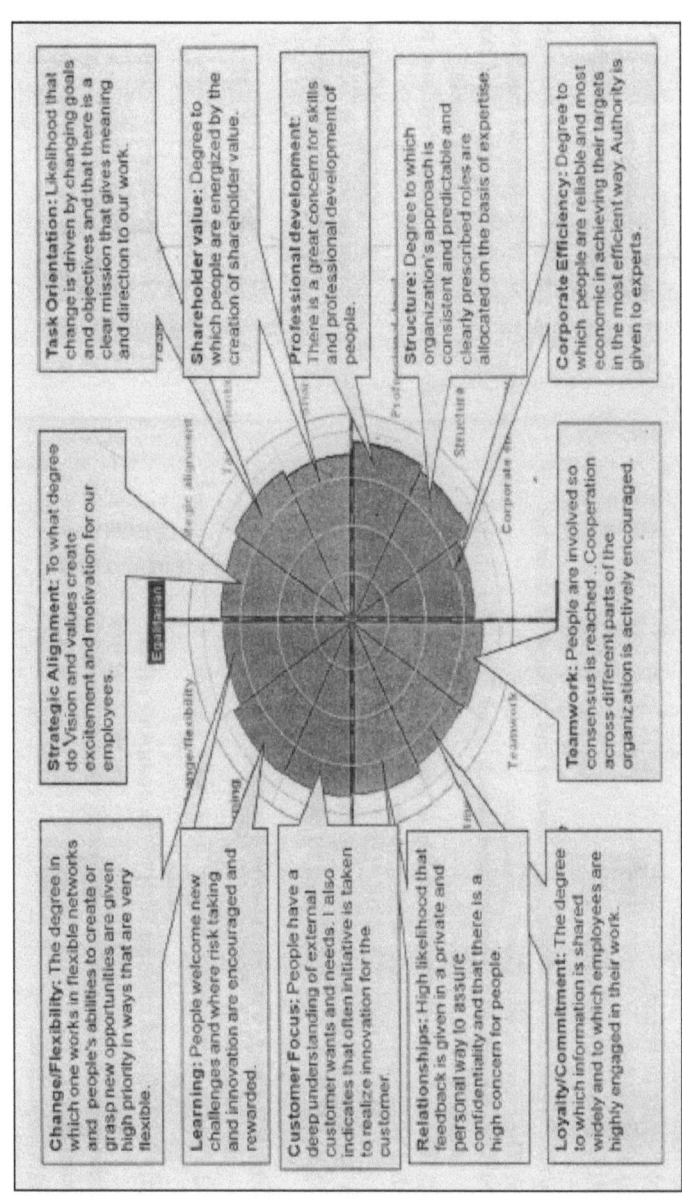

Appendix F

Integration Manager Profile & Tasks

Roles and Tasks of an Integration Manager:

(Schuler, 2001, p. 246)

- Project Manager, Communicator, Advisor, Advocate, Relationship Builder, Facilitator, Team Leader, Negotiator
- Putting the chaos in order, getting early results

Profile of an Integration Manager:

(Ashkenas, 2000, pp. 181-204)

- Deep knowledge of the acquiring company
- No need for credit: being tough and unbending with managers, staff, particularly about deadlines or coming decisions versus being a listener
- Comfort with chaos: motivating, involving people also by inspiring to become committed to the new organization and by making the process exciting; keeping the process moving by recalibrating plans, taking initiatives and making independent judgments
- Responsible independence: knowing when to check with the right people making sure things are moving in the right direction
- Emotional and cultural intelligence: appreciating emotional and cultural issues, managing them personally, helping deal with them constructively, providing a critical counterbalance

Appendix G

Cross-Cultural Training Content – example

(Source: Communicaid, 2011, p. 7)

- Cultural awareness: doing business, living & working, working successfully & negotiating across cultures
- Foreign language training: world languages, industry specifics, language testings
- Leadership and management: building international teams, developing global competence, managing virtual teams, effective global leadership

Appendix H

Trust Building Checklist

(Source: Covey, 2011)

1) Credibility through:
   - Integrity
   - Intent
   - Capabilities
   - Results

2) Relationship trust through behaviors:
   - Talk straight
   - Demonstrate respect
   - Create transparency
   - Right words
   - Show loyalty
   - Deliver results
   - Get better
   - Confront reality
   - Clarify expectations
   - Practice accountability
   - Listen first
   - Keep commitments
   - Extent trust

3) Organizational trust through alignment:
   - Increasing organizational integrity
   - Improving organizational intent
   - Increasing organizational capabilities
   - Improving organizational results

4) Market trust through reputation

5) Societal trust through contribution

Appendix I

Reconciling Dilemmas

(Source: Trompenaars, 2010, p. 41)

- Identifying the dilemma
- Charting the dilemma, labeling the axes reflecting the opposing positions
- Describing positive and negative sides of the dilemma
- Making epithets characterizing the sweet or sour of each side
- Asking how value A can support value B and vice versa
- Developing an action plan for recognizing potential obstacles and plan for monitoring

References

Achleitner, Ann-Kristin; Henselmann, Klaus (2012): Gabler Wirtschaftslexikon. Due Diliegence - Definition. Springer. Available online at http://wirtschaftslexikon.gabler.de/Archiv/9219/due-diligence-v9.html, updated on 22/06/2012, checked on 22/06/2012.

Ashkenas, Ronald N.; Francis, Suzanne C. (2000): Integration Managers. Special Leaders for Special Times. In *Harvard Business Review* 78 (6), pp. 108–116, checked on 11/06/2012.

Bech, Allan; Jeppesen, Kenneth (2007): Domestic and Crossborder M&As by European Acquirers. An investigation of performance and performance drivers in a short and long-term perspective. Aarhus School of Business, checked on 7/04/2012.

Bekier, Matthias M.; Bogardus, Anna J.; Oldham, Tim (2001): Why mergers fail. In *The McKinsey Quarterly* (4). Available online at https://www.mckinseyquarterly.com/Why_mergers_fail_1113, checked on 17/06/2012.

Bower, Joseph L. (2001): Not All M&As Are Alike and That Matters. In *Harvard Business Review* Vol. 79 (3), pp. 92–101, checked on 7/04/2012.

Carey, Dennis (2001): Harvard business review on mergers and acquisitions -. Lessons from Master Acquirers. Boston, Mass: Harvard Business School Press.

Carleton, J. Robert; Lineberry, Claude S. (2004): Achieving post-merger success. A stakeholder's guide to cultural due diligence, assessment, and integration. San Francisco: Pfeiffer.

Cartwright, Sue; Cooper, Cary L. (1996): Managing mergers, acquisitions, and strategic alliances. Integrating people and cultures. 2nd ed. Oxford; Boston: Butterworth-Heinemann.

Communicaid (2011): Cross-Border Mergers & Acquisitions. Reducing the Risk of Failure, checked on 1/04/2012.

Cottin, Andrew; Rehm, Werner; Uhlaner, Robert (2011): Growing through deals: a reality check. In *McKinsey Quarterly*. Available online at https://www.mckinseyquarterly.com/Growing_through_deals_A_reality_check_2793, checked on 17/06/2012.

Covey, Stephen M. R. (2010): The speed of trust. The one thing that changes everything. [Hamilton, N.Z.]: Summaries.Com.

Deutsch, Clay; West, Andy; McLetchie, James; Engert, Oliver; Rosiello, Rob; Kelly, Eileen (2010): Perspectives on Merger Integration. Available online at http://www.mckinsey.com/Client_Service/Organization/Latest_thinking/MM_compendium, checked on 17/06/2012.

Drori, Israel; Wrzesniewski, Amy; Ellis, Shmuel (2011): Cultural clashes in a "merger of equals": The case of high-tech start-ups. In *Hum. Resour. Manage* 50 (5), pp. 625–649, checked on 22/06/2012.

Faber, Ralf T. (2007): The human element. The impact of mergers and acquisitions on organizations and people.

Gerds, Johannes; Strottmann, Freddy (2010): Post Merger Integration: Hard Data, Hard Truths. In *Deloitte Review* (6). Available online at http://www.deloitte.com/view/de_DE/de/search/index.htm?searchKeywordsField=post+merger+integration+hard+data&searchKeywordsFieldDefault=Suche&searchBtn.x=0&searchBtn.y=0, checked on 17/06/2012.

Gitelson, Gene; Bing, John (2001): CULTURE SHOCK. In *CMA Management* 75 (1), pp. 40–44, checked on 11/06/2012.

Harding, David; Rovit, Sam (2004): Building Deals on Bedrock. In *Harvard Business Review* Vol. 82 (9), pp. 121–128, checked on 7/04/2012.

Hofstede, Geert H. (2001): Culture's consequences. Comparing values, behaviors, institutions, and organizations across nations. 2nd ed. Thousand Oaks, Calif: Sage Publications.

Knechtel, Cristian; Menzler, Thomas; Schick, Hatto; Spee, Margarethe von (2009): Post Merger Integration Study 2009. Ziegerade oder Achterbahn? Available online at http://www.imaa-institute.org/docs/m&a/pwc_13_post%20merger%20integration%20study%202009.pdf?PHPSESSID=6bfa4fa04e4caa9d75ddf8c4de43ee2f, checked on 17/06/2012.

KPMG (1999): Unlocking Shareholder Value: The Keys To Success. Mergers & Acquisitions. A Global Research Report, checked on 1/04/2012.

KPMG (2008): All To Play For. Striving for post deal success, checked on 1/04/2012.

KPMG (2011): A new dawn: good deals in challenging times, checked on 1/04/2012.

Krug, Jeffrey A. (2003): Why Do They Keep Leaving? In *Harvard Business Review* Vol. 81 (2), pp. 14–15, checked on 7/04/2012.

MarketLine (2011): Through mergers and aquisitions to success -. A marketline case study - Glaxo Smith Kline, checked on 22/06/2012.

mergermarket (2012): M&A Round-up for Year End 2011, pp. 1–53. Available online at http://www.mergermarket.com/pdf/Press-Release-for-Financial-Advisers-Year-End-2011.pdf, checked on 17/06/2012.

Piekkari, Rebecca; Vaara, Eero; Tienari, Janne; Säntti, Risto (2005): Integration or disintegration? Human resource implications of a common corporate language decision in a cross-border merger. In *The International Journal of Human Resource Management* 16 (3), pp. 330–344, checked on 11/06/2012.

Rehm, Werner; Uhlaner, Robert; West, Andy (2012): Taking a longer-term look at M&A value creation. In *McKinsey Quarterly*. Available online at https://www.mckinseyquarterly.com/Taking_a_longer-term_look_at_MA_value_creation_2916, checked on 17/06/2012.

Schein, Edgar H. (2004): Organizational culture and leadership. 3rd ed. San Francisco: Jossey-Bass.

Schneck, Ottmar (2007): Cultural Due Diligence oder warum die meisten Fusionen scheitern. In *Kredit & Ratingpraxis* (4), pp. 23–29, checked on 1/04/2012.

Schuler, Randall; Jackson, Susan (2001): HR Issues and Activities in Mergers & Acquisitions. In *European Management Journal* Vol. 19 (3), pp. 239–253, checked on 1/04/2012.

Trompenaars, Fons; Nijhoff Asser, Maarten (2010): The Global M & A Tango. How to Reconcile Cultural Differences in Mergers, Acquisitions and Strategic Partnerships. Oxford: Infinite Ideas Ltd.

Wollersheim, Jutta; Barthel, Erich (2008): Kulturunterschiede bei Mergers & Acquisitions: Entwicklung eines Konzeptes zur Durchführung einer Cultural Due Diligence. Frankfurt School of Finance & Management - Working Paper Series (94).

Zhu, Zhanwen; Huang, Haifeng (2007): The Cultural Integration in the Process of Cross-border Mergers & Acquisitions 3 (2), pp. 40–44. Available online at http://www.usimr.org/IMR-2-2007/v3n207-art5.pdf, checked on 22/06/2012.

Other Bibliography

Aiello, Robert J.; Watkins, Michael D. (2000): The Fine Art of Friendly Acquisition. In *Harvard Business Review* 78 (6), pp. 100–107, checked on 11/06/2012.

Ashkenas, Ronald N.; Demonaco, Lawrence J.; Francis, Suzanne C. (1998): Making the Deal Real: How GE Capital Integrates Acquisitions. In *Harvard Business Review* 76 (1), pp. 165–178, checked on 11/06/2012.

Baldacchino, Godfrey (1997): A clash of human resource management cultures: a micro-state case study. In *International Journal of Human Resource Management* 8 (4), pp. 506–518, checked on 11/06/2012.

Christensen, Clayton M.; Alton, Richard; Rising, Curtis; Waldeck, Andrew (2011): The Big Idea - The new M&A Playbook. Why you should pay top dollar for a "killer deal"—and other new rules for making acquisitions Vol. 89 (3), pp. 48–57, checked on 24/03/2012.

Cliffe, Sarah (1999): Can This Merger Be Saved? In *Harvard Business Review* 77 (1), pp. 28–44, checked on 11/06/2012.

Cogman, David; Sivertsen, Carsten Buch (2011): A return to deal making in 2010. In *McKinsey Quarterly*. Available online at https://www.mckinseyquarterly.com/A_return_to_deal_making_in_2010_2727, checked on 17/06/2012.

Eccles, Robert G.; Lanes, Kersten L.; Wilson, Thomas C. (1999): Are You Paying Too Much for That Acquisition? In *Harvard Business Review* 77 (4), pp. 136–146, checked on 11/06/2012.

Harding, David; Rouse, Ted (2007): Human Due Diligence. In *Harvard Business Review* Vol. 85 (4), pp. 124–131, checked on 1/04/2012.

KPMG (2008): Doing Deals in Tough Times. Best Practices of Leading M&A Teams, checked on 1/04/2012.

KPMG (2011): The Determinants of M&A Success. What Factors Contribute to Deal Sucess?, checked on 1/04/2012.

Kramer, Roderick M. (2009): Rethinking Trust. In *Harvard Business Review* Vol. 87 (6), pp. 68–77, checked on 1/04/2012.

Light, David A. (2001): Who Goes, Who Stays? In *Harvard Business Review* 79 (1), pp. 34–44, checked on 11/06/2012.

Page, Nick; Johansson, Fredrik (2011): Sharing Deal Insight. European Financial Services M&A news and views, checked on 1/04/2012.

Palm, Andreas (2011): Konzepte zur Kulturellen Integration nach M&A (13), checked on 22/06/2012.

Pursche, Bill (2001): Do most mergers really fail? Available online at http://www.firstcalladvisors.com/Articles.html, checked on 17/06/2012.

Rappaport, Alfred; Sirower, Mark L. (1999): Stock or Cash? The Trade-Offs for Buyers and Sellers in Mergers and Acquisition. In *Harvard Business Review* 77 (6), pp. 147–158, checked on 11/06/2012.

Sivertsen, Carsten Buch (2012): A mixed year for M&A. In *McKinsey Quarterly*. Available online at https://www.mckinseyquarterly.com/A_mixed_year_for_MA_2917, checked on 17/06/2012.

Wolf, Renita (2003): INTEGRATION. Key to M&A Success. In *Financial Executive* 19 (6), pp. 62–64, checked on 11/06/2012